Yesterday and Today in Hudson

Ray Lennard

To Carol – Enjoy!

a publication of
W. G. Thompson House Museum, Hudson, Michigan

YESTERDAY: In the early 1980s while cleaning out the third story of the Adrian Laundry, Jack Lennard discovered cartons of glass plate negatives. Several of the images appeared to be of the Lenawee County area. After further research, Dr. Charles Lindquist of the Lenawee County Historical Museum discovered they were of the Hudson, Michigan area. The images, dating from the late 1890s through 1900, were thanks to an amateur camera club, whose members pose here.

photo courtesy of Lenawee County Historical Museum

photo courtesy of Ray Lennard

TODAY: Ray Lennard, curator of the W. G. Thompson House Museum in Hudson, poses here with his wife Kara. The Thompson House Museum opened in September 2005 and is dedicated to the preservation of not only the home and collections of William G. Thompson and his family, but the interests of Mr. Thompson, including Hudson's rich and historic past.

YESTERDAY: In 1833, the area around what would become Hudson, Michigan, was an unbroken wilderness. Early in the year, Hiram Kidder and a group of land prospectors entered the area and began staking out claims. To encourage settlement, Kidder "played up" the assets of the area, including the incredible power of the Tiffin River, or as it is known locally, "Bean Creek." Kidder and other settlers began clearing the area in October 1833.

TODAY: View of the "mighty" Bean Creek during the summer of 2010 as viewed from atop the old Cincinnati and Northern Railroad bridge over the Tiffin River. It is hard for modern-day viewers of the lazy stream to see the potential power of the water . . . however, without the creek, Hudson may never have been here!

YESTERDAY: The Van Akin family constructed this dam on the Tiffin River north of Hudson to harness the power of the water to power the family sawmill. The Van Akins, among the first settlers in the Bean Creek area, opened one of the first sawmills in the area, helping farmers to clear the land and providing lumber to the growing area.

TODAY: View of the Van Akin mill area, located on the southeast side of Kiel Highway and Beecher Road. Little if any traces of the dam and mill remain today. Those with a vivid imagination could conceive the boulder in the center of the River to be part of the original dam's structure.

YESTERDAY: Shortly after Michigan's statehood, the legislature authorized the construction of a railroad that would link Monroe to New Buffalo. The first leg of the new railway ran from Monroe to Adrian, and was completed in 1837. The state-authorized railroad soon ran out of funding; however, it would be purchased by a group of private investors. Seeking the best route to New Buffalo, the investors called for proposals from the communities as to how the tracks should be laid. Hudson convinced the company of the potential for the area and in May 1843 the first engine arrived in Hudson. The Lakeshore and Michigan Southern Railroad depot construction began in 1885 and opened for passenger traffic in 1886.

photo courtesy of Kara Lennard

TODAY: Railroad travel gave way to automobile travel in the 1950s. By the 1960s, the depot stood vacant as the New York Central Railroad Company suspended passenger trains through Hudson. Rumors of a street-widening project for Railroad Street threatened the depot. A small group of concerned Hudson citizens rallied to try and save the depot from the wrecking ball. In 1971, they lost the battle and the depot rubble now sits in the bottom of "Sauerkraut Lake." Today the depot's lot is an empty grassy area.

YESTERDAY: Image of the single-span stone arch Lakeshore and Michigan Southern Railroad bridge over the Tiffin River. Constructed in 1871 by the L&MSRR, the stone bridge replaced the wooden trussed structure built in 1843. The massive structure measures seventy-five feet long and forty-two feet wide, and spans sixty-five feet. The locally quarried stone is finished in an ashlar cutting method. The bridge made up part of the original sixty-six miles of the Lakeshore and Michigan Southern Railroad track, linking Monroe to Hillsdale.

photo courtesy of Ray Lennard

TODAY: The bridge today is one of Hudson's most recognizable landmarks. In 2008, a group of citizens led by longtime railroad buff James Findlay secured a Michigan Historical Marker for the structure. In addition, the stone arch bridge is listed on the State of Michigan's Register of Historic Places for its "outstanding size" and its "excellent state of repair."

YESTERDAY: The power house of the Hudson Milling Company, as viewed from under the stone arch railroad bridge. The industriously constructed power house used the waterpower of the Tiffin River via a mill race channel constructed a mile and a half upriver. The mill race carried the water to the power house and turned the waterwheel inside the structure, which in turn moved the belt flywheel. A careful eye can see the massive cable belt that links the power house's pulleys to the Mill House's pulleys.

TODAY: Today's view of the power house area. The area adjacent and behind the railroad bridge serves the city as a walking trail. The powerhouse is long gone, and has been replaced by woody growth.

YESTERDAY: By the 1860s, Hudson became a thriving area on the western edge of Lenawee County. This view taken from the east side of town captures the twin bridges over the Tiffin River. The Lakeshore and Michigan Southern Railroad transported the many agricultural products from the Hudson area, including fruit, grains, and wool. Businesses in Hudson produced harnesses, carriages, spokes, and other goods for markets in Detroit, New York, and Chicago.

TODAY: The same view today. Hudson's economy has undergone many changes since 1860, but it remains a manufacturer of parts for businesses and industry in Detroit, Chicago, and points beyond.

YESTERDAY: Main Street Hudson in the 1930s. Note the electric company storefront on Main Street. George Avis settled in Hudson in the 1880s. Short on money but filled with ambition, Avis would start an electrical generating plant of steam in Hudson during the 1890s. By the 1900s, the plant powered all of Hudson and most of the surrounding area. Avis's steam plant became the envy of an electric company in Jackson, Michigan. Consumers Power purchased the plant from Avis and immediately doubled the size of its company and its energy production.

TODAY: Downtown Hudson today. Hudson's historic downtown boasts fifty architecturally significant structures of many types, including locally fired brick and frame. The storefronts show the skills of local construction workers as cast iron storefronts, stone carvings, elaborate moldings, and other decorative facades grace the buildings. While some of the lower levels of the storefronts have been modified from their original appearance, the majority of the upper floors retain their original features.

YESTERDAY: View of the northwest corner of Main and Church streets. The photographer likely set up his camera in the window of Oren Howe's dry goods store. The photographer captured one of the few images of the original location of the Congregational Church in Hudson. The structure would later be moved to face Lane Street and operated as the Opera House.

TODAY: Modern view of the northwest corner of Main and Church Streets. The building on the corner served for many years as Meyer's Department Store. Today Subway and consignment stores share the space. The Congregational Church lot has a typical 1880s block storefront.

YESTERDAY: A view of the east side of Church Street, looking south from the corner of Railroad and Church. The most identifiable landmark is the City Building in the center, with the bell tower. The City Council chambers occupied part of the structure, with the fire department filling the other half. In 1873, the city purchased a Troy fire bell to alert the volunteers to the threat of fire. In 1879, the city purchased a new steam-powered fire engine to occupy the building.

TODAY: The same view today. The city demolished the old City Building in 1973 for a municipal parking lot.

YESTERDAY: 1880s view of the east side of Church Street looking south from the corner of Church and Railroad streets. The most notable building is the Hudson Hotel and Livery, situated on the left of the image.

TODAY: Same view today. The Hudson Hotel burned in 1966, making way for a new City Hall located on the southeast corner of Church and Railroad.

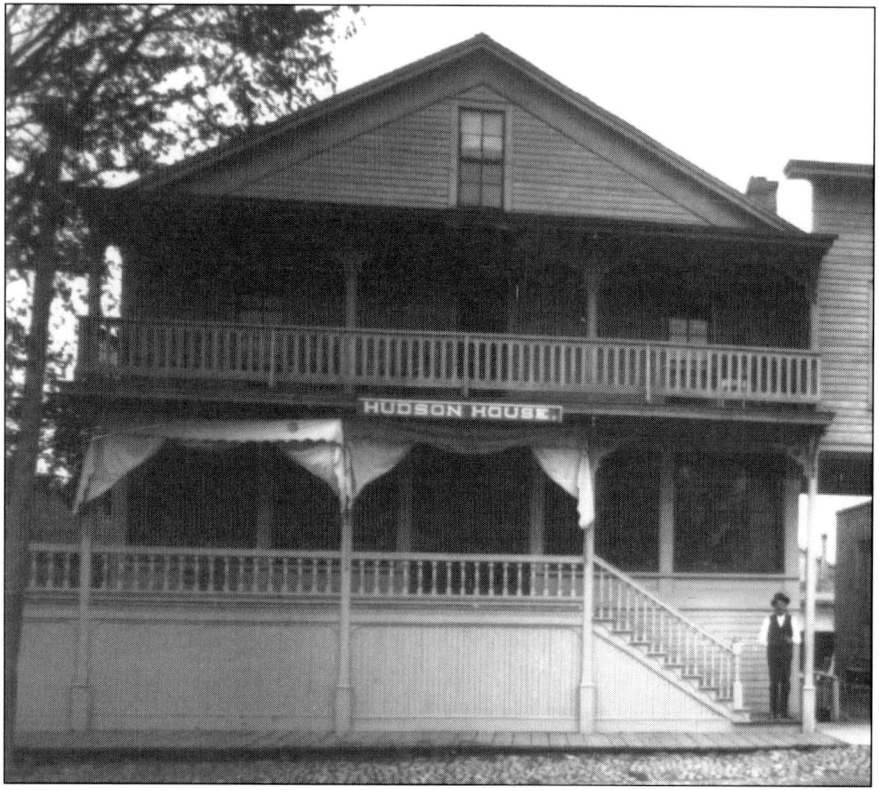

photo courtesy of Lenawee County Historical Museum

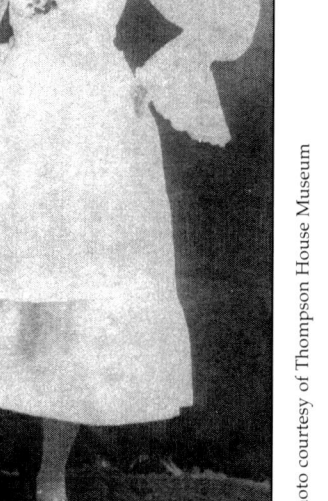

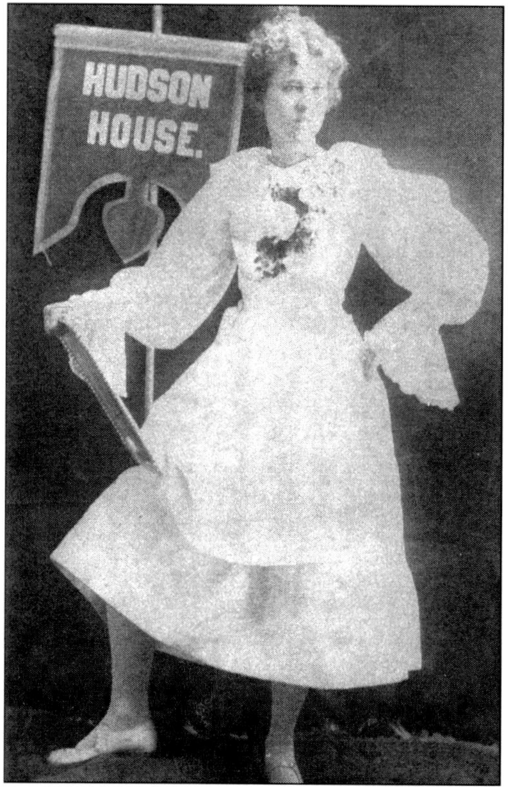

photo courtesy of Thompson House Museum

YESTERDAY: The Hudson House Hotel, located on North Church Street. The business featured rooms for rent, a dining room, and a livery. A. H. Lane and his family ran the business until the 1920s, when it sold to Fred Britten and Elizabeth Way. At right is a lovely lady advertising the Hudson House Hotel, taken from an advertising card that dates to about 1900.

TODAY: Hudson's City Hall resides on the Hudson House Hotel property today. In 1966, the structure suffered a severe fire, making the building structurally unsound. A year later, the Lenawee County Fire Chief's Association burned the remaining building for training purposes. In 1968, the Hudson City Council authorized the construction of a new City Building.

YESTERDAY: An 1880s view of Brant's New Hotel, located at 114 N. Market Street. Rodney Whitehall opened this hotel in the 1870s. Shortly after its opening, Whitehall sold the operation to the Brant family (who are standing two in from the left of the image, by the corner of the porch).

TODAY: As automobile travel increased and train travel decreased in post-World War II America, hotels in Hudson faced a lack of business. In 1948, Brant's Hotel met with the wrecking ball. In its place, a bowling alley was built. Recently the structure served as a used book store.

YESTERDAY: View of the depot of the Cincinnati and Northern Railroad. In 1884, the Jackson and Ohio Railroad Company filed papers for the construction of a north/south railroad between the Ohio border and Jackson, Michigan. The ambitious plan soon ran short of funds and joined with a railroad company constructing a line from Cincinnati, Ohio. The merged line became known as the Cincinnati, Jackson, and Mackinaw Railroad, which finished the line in May 1887.

TODAY: View of the depot area today. The financially plagued rail line was a popular way for passengers from Hudson to travel to Jackson, but the bulk of the freight from Hudson left via the Lake Shore and Michigan Southern line. In 1938, the line sold to Norfolk and Southern, who closed the line in the 1950s.

YESTERDAY: Lake Shore and Michigan Southern Railroad over then "M-14," north of M-34.

TODAY: Modern view of the same area. The State of Michigan razed the structure in 1971 to make way for improvements to the newly renamed US-127.

YESTERDAY: Pearl Laundry, located on North Church Street across from the then Hudson Hotel, circa 1890.

TODAY: The Pearl Laundry structure, today a private residence.

YESTERDAY: Thompson Savings Bank views, top showing the bank around 1890. In 1867, Gamaliel Thompson and William Thompson entered into partnership with John Osborn, Martin Perkins, and William Ames to start the Savings Bank of Osborn, Perkins & Co. The name became Thompson Savings Bank around 1892, when the State of Michigan reorganized its banking laws. In the image, the young boy is William R. Thompson, second generation bank president. The interior photo of the bank dates to 1917. In the center left is a grown William R. Thompson, and center right is G. I. Thompson.

photo courtesy of Kara Lennard

TODAY: The old Thompson Savings Bank today. The façade of the bank underwent modernization in the 1920s, giving the building its current appearance. In the 1960s, Thompson Savings Bank built a new structure a quarter-mile west of this site. In the 1980s, the bank along with M&S Manufacturing deeded the structure to the city of Hudson to open the Hudson Historical Museum.

YESTERDAY: J. A. Dillion, Jr. Implements sold farm machinery and goods to the farmers of the greater Hudson area from the 1880s up through the Great Depression in the 1930s. Located on Main Street west of the Bean Creek, it was a popular stop when the farm families came to Hudson.

TODAY: In the 1960s, Dillion Implements made way for new industry. Metalloy Foundry demolished the old structure to make way for a new factory building. The site today is owned by a private individual.

YESTERDAY: Advertisement card for Philip Seewald's jewelry store taken around 1885. Phillip Seewald came to America from the Bavarian province of Germany in 1833. A skilled jeweler and clock repairer, he passed the love of fine jewelry to his son, John Phillip Seewald. The pair came to Hudson in 1874 and opened the Seewald Jewelry Store, located on Main Street. The store was known not only for its jewelry and watches, but for its fine silver products, as shown in this card.

photo courtesy of Thompson House Museum

photo courtesy of Thompson House Museum

TODAY: Modern-day view of the town clock, which stands directly in front of the old Seewald Jewelry Store. Built by skilled German watchmaker Phillip Seewald and his son John Phillip in 1859, the clock was housed in a church tower at Freemont, Ohio before being brought to Hudson in 1874. The works of the clock reside in the basement of the old jewelry store. Five hundred pound weights drive the clock mechanism, which sprawls out under the sidewalk to the base of the clock. Five generations of Seewalds wound the clock and cared for it. In 1931, Henry C. Blanks became proprietor and responsibility for the clock's care continued during his lifetime and over the succeeding years by his son, Charles. In 1982, the iconic clock become property of the city of Hudson.

YESTERDAY: The W. H. Abbott Auto Garage and Machine Shop, located on the north side of Main street west of the Tiffin River, was one of the first automotive repair shops in Hudson. Cars came to Hudson in the 1900's, and according to Thompson lore, G. I. Thompson (builder of the structure which is now the Thompson House Museum) owned the first car in town, a nine passenger Lincoln touring auto. The suppiles for the car had to be brought in via rail . . . including gasoline!

photo courtesy of Thompson House Museum

photo courtesy of Ray Lennard

TODAY: The current view of Abbott's garage. Today the building serves as storage for one of the local auto parts stores.

YESTERDAY: Image of the Hudson Milling Company Building, taken around 1885. The mill occupied both sides of Main Street by Bean Creek (those with a keen eye can see the stone arch bridge to the right of the Milling Company building). A key business within the Hudson Community, the Mill provided a way for local grains to be ground into flour and shipped to the cities of Chicago and Detroit.

TODAY: The area of the Hudson Milling Company today. Hudson Milling's building became obsolete and the site was favorable for Rima to develop an industrial site here. Rima then sold the building to Metaloy. Upon Metaloy's closing, the site lay vacant, and it is now home to Main Street Florist and the Hudson Cinema.

YESTERDAY: The view of Fernsdorf's wool house. The building actually started its life as the home of the Free Will Baptist Church, constructed in 1858. When the Baptists left the building, the facility became the Presbyterian Church. Eventually the old building was no longer fit for human use. Seeing an opportunity, Louis Fernsdorf used the aged structure to store his wool for market.

TODAY: The site of the church/wool house today. The structure was removed in the 1940s and this new home was built.

YESTERDAY: M. E. Caner's Market, located on the northwest corner of Main and Market streets. The long-lived store opened in 1855 and was sold in 1930 after seventy-four years in the same family.

TODAY: The northwest corner of Main and Market streets today. A devastating fire in the 1980s destroyed two buildings in downtown Hudson, including the old Caner's Market. Today the lot serves as informal parking for downtown businesses.

YESTERDAY: The Helvetica Milk plant, from a 1910 postcard. The plant, located on Mechanic Street near the Cincinnati Northern Railroad Depot, originated in 1909. Buying milk for $1.55 per one hundred pounds, the factory produced evaporated milk. At its peak of production during World War I, the company boasted nearly two hundred workers. Business was so good that the operators actually opened an annex that produced the cans for canning the milk.

TODAY: The area of the Helvetica Milk Plant today. In 1924, the Helvetica Company merged with another firm to become the Pet Milk Factory. During the Great Depression, the company shuttered the milk factory and ran only the can lines. As pasteurization became the standard process for marketing milk, the plant closed in 1949.

YESTERDAY: The Kellogg Harness factory and livery stable display during the Hudson Street Fair, likely 1890. The Kellogg building peeks over the top of the display tent, which is showing off the latest in harnesses and carriage technology. The building, erected in 1871, served as a meeting place for the Odd Fellows (who used the second floor).

photo courtesy of Kara Lennard

TODAY: The Kellogg building today. Today it serves as a karate studio. Next door is the Bi-County Herald office.

YESTERDAY: City of Hudson's water treatment plant as it appeared near the time of its opening in 1890.

TODAY: Hudson's water treatment center today.

YESTERDAY: With the completion of the waterworks in 1890, the city moved to hook up the residences of the city with water. Here, workers run the water main up Oak Street around 1891.

TODAY: Oak Street today.

photo courtesy of Ray Lennard

YESTERDAY: The Hudson Public Library from a postcard dated 1910. The library came to be when Byron Foster wrote a request to Andrew Carnegie in early 1903. Mr. Carnegie replied on March 27, 1903, agreeing to furnish $10,000 as long as the city found a suitable building site and agreed to maintain the structure as a free library. Claire Allen of Jackson, Michigan designed the building and the Koch Brothers of Ann Arbor constructed the massive stone structure. The building opened in 1905.

photo courtesy of Thompson House Museum

TODAY: The Hudson Public Library today. The interior of the structure has been extensively remodeled, adding an elevator and additional shelving units. It is a popular place for all ages, especially during the warm summer months. Regular story times keep children entertained and the Internet computers are always full. Books still are the main focus of the library. When the library first opened, it boasted a catalogue of two thousand volumes. Today, the library houses over forty-five thousand books and can request books from across the nation!

YESTERDAY: Maple Grove Cemetery as it appeared in the late 1880s. The cemetery was not always located at the end of Maple Grove. In the 1830s, the Hudson's departed rested in the cemetery plot where Webster's Park currently is. By the 1860s, this small tract of land became full, and the need for a new cemetery began a great debate in Hudson's papers and in Council chambers. In 1867, the Hudson Village Council on behalf of the Cemetery Society acquired fifteen acres of land located upon the farm of Samuel Pittenger. The acreage on a hill was located at a high point in town; it would become known as the "New Cemetery" and would be named Maple Grove Cemetery.

TODAY: A view of Maple Grove today. The parklike setting of the Victorian cemetery makes it an excellent place to walk and jog while reflecting upon the lives of Hudsonites long gone.

YESTERDAY: The receiving vault at Maple Grove Cemetery c. 1880. For many years, the cemetery sextons had to hold caskets in storage prior to burial during the winter months when it was not possible to dig in the frozen ground. In 1881, voters approved the building of a receiving vault, at a cost of $1,000, and this was completed around 1884, the structure measuring 16 x 16 feet with 14-inch walls. The vault, designed by Adrian Architect, C. F. Matthes, is ornamental in style and served as a receiving vault for many years.

TODAY: The vault remains today, but is now used for storage, though retains its distinctive style.

photo courtesy of Kara Lennard

YESTERDAY: One of the more unusual monuments in Maple Grove Cemetery marks the resting place of L. R. Pierson. A staunch atheist, Pierson had the following inscribed on his gravestone: "FELLOW PILGRIM, Help in trouble, if you can get it, comes from Nature, Humanity, Knowledge, here on this Earth, nowhere else. Think of it. L.R. Pierson, Attorney at Law, Hudson, Mich. No Charges."

photo courtesy of Lenawee County Historical Museum

photo courtesy of Kara Lennard

TODAY: According to Hudson lore, the family struck the inscription from the monument after his death.

YESTERDAY: Images captured by the camera club of early Hudson dwellings, circa the late 1880s. While the actual location within the city of Hudson is a mystery, the homes are typical of those built by settlers to the area. Miraculously, the structures survived two major fires that nearly burned Hudson to the ground, the first occurring in 1858 and the second happening in 1864.

TODAY: The Trask house, built in 1844. The Trask family came from Massachusetts in 1835. Purported to be the first wood-framed structure in the city, it is rumored that its structure rests upon the foundation of one of the first log cabins built in what would become the city of Hudson. It is likely that this building is the oldest structure in Hudson.

YESTERDAY: Constructed in the early 1840s, the Lorenzo Palmer house is also known as the George Williams home. Mr. Williams moved from Hillsdale County to Hudson in the 1850s. Mr. Williams's daughter Sophia married G. I. Thompson and lived in another notable Hudson home, the Thompson House, which now is a museum.

TODAY: The Palmer house as it appears today. The structure has undergone a complete remodeling, including the addition of modern kitchen. Still, the structure is a remarkable Greek Revival architectural example. The iconic six-over-six windows on the upper level and the locally crafted Ionic columns remain after more than one hundred and fifty years.

YESTERDAY: The G. I. Thompson residence located at 101 Summit Street. Construction began on the future residence for G. I. and Sophia Thompson in early 1890. The total cost of the structure topped out at $6,500! The three-story home contained all the modern convinces available at the time, including closets, a forced-air coal-fired furnace, and a split water system featuring city drinking water and cistern-collected washing water.

photo courtesy of Thompson House Museum

TODAY: The structure as it appears today. William G. Thompson, the last member of the Thompson Family in Hudson, requested the home with contents to be opened as a historic house museum. Opening in 2005, the W. G. Thompson House Museum and Gardens hosts over four hundred visitors each year and offers monthly programs on a wide variety of topics to educate and entertain Hudsonites.

YESTERDAY: John K. Boies ordered this stately home to be erected in 1862. Boies came to Hudson in 1845 and opened a mercantile with his brother. The business expanded as Hudson grew, and by the 1850s the firm sold farmers' produce as well as dry goods. In 1855, Boies formed the Exchange Bank with the assistance of his brother and Nathan Rude. After Boies' death in 1891, the home sold to C. B. Stowell. Stowell modernized the structure, including adding the massive porch, library bookcases, and stained glass windows.

TODAY: The Boies/Stowell house as it appears today. In 1930, the home came into the possession of the Narrance family, who organized and operated a home for mentally handicapped girls. Today the Coleman family operates the Coleman Foundation out of the stately home. The Foundation continues to assist mentally handicapped females.

photo courtesy of Lenawee County Historical Museum

YESTERDAY: Built in 1891 by Edwin H. Cogswell, this stately Queen Anne-style home sat on Main Street in Hudson. Mr. Cogswell, a person in the lumber wholesale business, used only the finest materials in his home, including red oak, white oak, birdseye maple, birch, cherry, and walnut. The home also featured fine stained glass windows, marble fixtures, and curved plate glass windows. Upon the death of Mr. Cogswell, the home passed on to Floyd Avis, the operator of the municipal electric power company in Hudson.

TODAY: The site of the Cogswell house today. In the 1960s, Thompson Savings Bank acquired the property, looking to create a more suitable building for modern banking practices. W. G. Thompson, president of Thompson Savings bank, ordered the removal and preservation of the historic features of the Cogswell house and tasked an architect with incorporating the old woodwork and stained glass into the modern bank. The result is a unique bank interior that still serves the community today.

YESTERDAY: The Chamberlain house, located Seward Street in Hudson. This picturesque home is built in the Gothic Cottage style of architecture. The home, built in the late 1860s, stood between Howard and Grove Streets.

photo courtesy of Lenawee County Historical Museum

TODAY: The likely site of the Chamberlain House today. Dr. and Mrs. Lowell Blanchard built this brick Tudor Revival style home on a double lot in the 1950s. It is unknown when the Chamberlain home succumbed to the wrecking ball.

YESTERDAY: Workers pause while installing windows on the home of Nathan Rude. This photograph captures the completion of the Rude home, around 1876. The distinctive structure features curved glass windows and imported Italian marble fireplaces. Mr. Rude, along with the Boies family, operated the Exchange Bank.

photo courtesy of Lenawee County Historical Museum

photo courtesy of Kara Lennard

TODAY: The Rude home as it appears today. In the 1930s, the property went to auction and came into the possession of Fred Culver. Mr. Culver planned to restore it; however, the structure sold to Taylor Dulworth and family. Soon thereafter, the home opened as the Collins real estate office. Today the home is multiplex apartments.

YESTERDAY: The Louis Fernsdorf house, located at the corner of Church and Railroad streets. This Queen Anne-style home featured sycamore woodwork in the lower floor rooms, including the music room, library, and smoking parlor. Fernsdorf emigrated from Germany at age eighteen, arriving in New York City. After drifting across New York and Ohio, he eventually settled in Hudson. Here he opened a grocery and provision store on Main Street. Through a "can do" attitude and serious study of American business practices and the English language, Fernsdorf became the predominate buyer of grain, wool, pork, hides, and produce in Michigan.

photo courtesy of Lenawee County Historical Museum

TODAY: The site of the Fernsdorf house today. The structure met with the wrecking ball in 1978. Notice the large side yard of the new structure. It is said that the massive foundation of the old house could not be removed, so the builders simply moved over the new house to accommodate building site conditions!

YESTERDAY: Hudson's West Side School around 1875. The land for the school lot was a donation from James Cobb. The site was a beautiful one for a school, especially considering the spacious lawn and playground area the large lot afforded. In 1891, the interior of the school building received extensive remodeling.

TODAY: The West Side School site as it appears today. In the 1960s, Hudson School District began construction on a new campus near the cemetery on Maple Grove. The old building met its end in 1982. New homes now dot the massive lot, though with a keen eye one still can see traces of the school, such as the old sidewalk drop-off area.

YESTERDAY: Photograph of Thompson Field, given to the city of Hudson by G. I. Thompson and his son W. R. Thompson in 1921. The old North Branch School on top of the hill, on West Street, and former location of DeGolyer Post, GAR, was concerted into showers and dressing rooms for the athletes. The grandstand was roofed over, and had screening in front of it.

TODAY: Thompson Field's bleachers as they appear today. The old bleachers have been removed, and the entire field reorganized for the playing of football, a serious sport in the city of Hudson. In 2009, the Hudson Tigers reached the State of Michigan finals in their class once again, losing to Traverse City St. Frances in the Division Seven group.

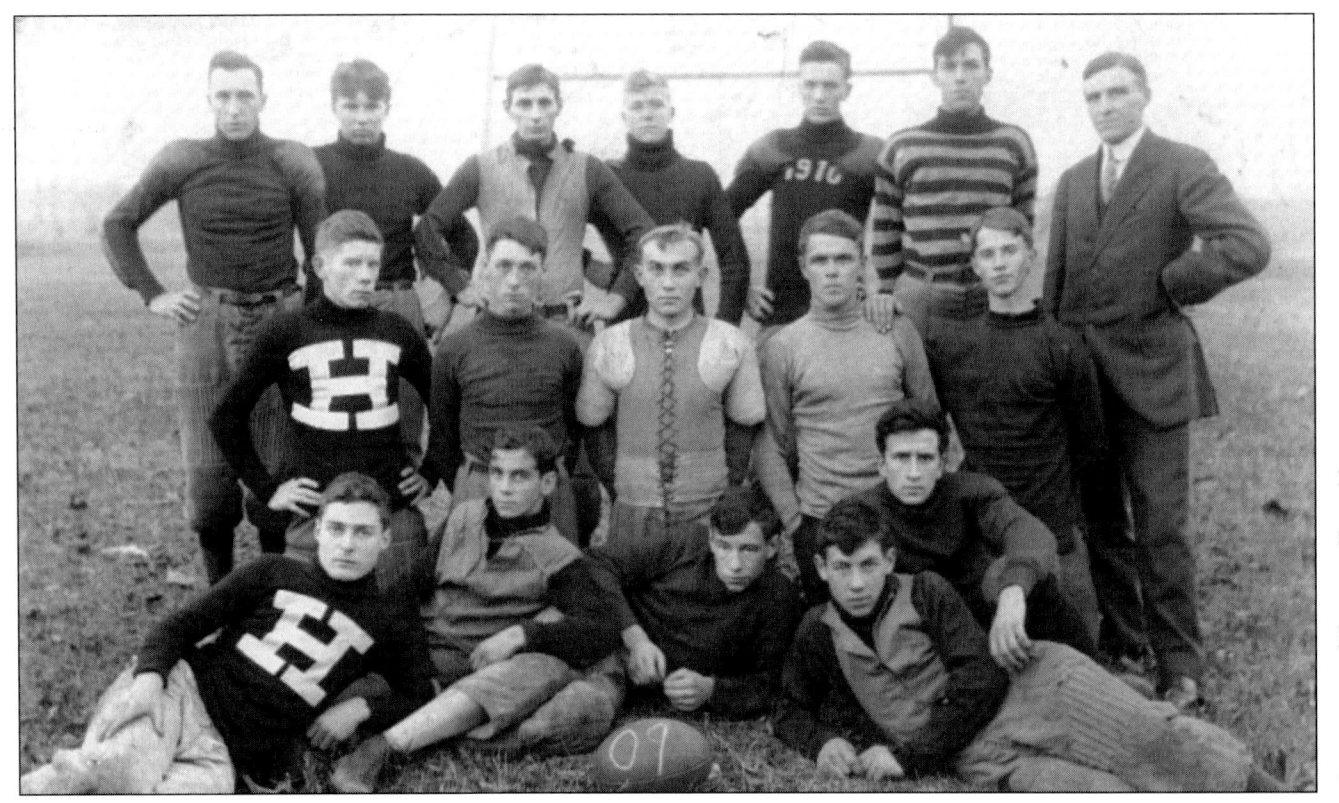

YESTERDAY: The 1909 Hudson High football team. Hudson was one of the first schools in the county to field a team, and scrimmaged the likes of Adrian College and Detroit College in the early days. Football remains a serious activity in Hudson Schools.

TODAY: The 1975 Hudson High School football team. The Hudson Tigers had the honor of having the longest winning streak in the United States during the 1970s. The seventy-two game winning streak placed Hudson Football and their coach Tom Saylor on the national stage. The record held until 1997 when Concord De La Salle of California eclipsed the mark, eventually winning 151 straight games.

YESTERDAY: Postcard view of the Congregational Church of Hudson. Built in 1871 at a cost of about $18,000, this marks the second location for the church. The original house of worship was located on Main Street. It is said that upon completion of the building, the pastor led the congregation on a march from the old house of worship to the new.

photo courtesy of Thompson House Museum

TODAY: Modern view of the Congregational Church. The steeple succumbed to a July 4, 1892 storm. The congregation only restored the lower portion of the steeple. In 2008, a much-needed street level entrance was added, and an elevator installed to allow for easier access to the pews.

YESTERDAY: Sacred Heart Catholic Church from a postcard dated 1910. Originally a church in Medina that served the large Irish Catholic settlement in the area, the church moved to the growing city in 1858, erecting a house of worship on the east side of Hudson at the corner of School and Spring streets. In 1904, the congregation voted to build a new structure. What resulted is this structure, dedicated on October 30, 1906 at an estimated cost of $60,000.

photo courtesy of Thompson House Museum

photo courtesy of Ray Lennard

TODAY: Modern view of the church. To the left one can see the rectory, completed a few years after the church. In addition, the church built a school across the street that serves several Hudson families.

YESTERDAY: Hudson's Methodist Church began with the first meeting in November 1835. At the top, the current Methodist church (c. 1898) replaced the aged structure located on the east side of Maple Grove, halfway between Hill and Wilcox streets. The new structure is constructed of cut fieldstone. Below, Methodist Sunday School members celebrate during the summer of 1917.

TODAY: A modern view of the Methodist Church. The Methodist Church boasts a strong, civic-minded congregation that is active in supporting Hudson.

YESTERDAY: In 1843, the Baptist Church of Christ in Hudson formed. Just four years later, the church members voted to erect a 32 x 44-foot building complete with steeple as their house of worship. The building site was in downtown Hudson, and stood just east of the current Hudson Museum. In 1851, a major fire consumed the Baptist church, as well as several other businesses and dwellings in the downtown area. Undeterred, the Baptists rebuilt their house of worship in its present location in 1852, as seen in this 1910s postcard. The building has undergone a few changes since the original construction. In 1867, needing more room, 25 feet was added to the south end of the church. A baptistery was added at a later date.

photo courtesy of Thompson House Museum

TODAY: The long-time Hudson Grange Fair ended in the 1980s, only to be replaced by the Bean Creek Festival. Held the second weekend in September, festival-goers can be assured of having fun on wild rides, seeing the wares of the local businesses, checking out crafts, and enjoying living in a small town.

YESTERDAY: Panoramic view of Hudson's skyline as taken from northwest of the city. Note the railroad bridge over what would become US-127, and the spire of the Congregational Church (center right) and the bell tower of city hall (center left).

photo courtesy of Lenawee County Historical Museum

photo courtesy of Ray Lennard

TODAY: A modern view of the Baptist Church. In 1959, the church's distinctive steeple was removed due to unsafe conditions. Interestingly, a few years before the steeple came down, another church in Hudson offered to "swap" buildings. Trinity Episcopal Church members approached the Baptist Church and offered an exchange of properties; the Baptists would move into Trinity and Trinity members would occupy the Baptist structure. Much deliberation ensued amongst the members of the Baptist Church. Finally, in mid-1954, the members of the Baptist Church decided to remain in their building and turn down the "church swap."

photos courtesy of the Hudson Museum

YESTERDAY: An artist's sketch of the proposed Trinity Episcopal Church. The Trinity Episcopal Church began in 1860, with members meeting at the home of Reverend Smythe. By 1872, membership grew to allow the congregation to engage in securing a house of worship. Erected in a gothic style, the brick structure showcased stained glass windows that depicted passages from the Bible, as well as tributes to important members of the parish. The original design called for the addition of a large tower to be built on the east side of the structure. Unfortunately, funds were not available for the construction of the elaborate steeple/tower structure.

Trinity Church could boast nearly two hundred members by 1900. As time marched forward, the membership would begin to dwindle. By the late 1940s, the church lacked a full-time, regular minister. In October 1953, Trinity Episcopal Church closed its doors.

photo courtesy of Ray Lennard

TODAY: The site of Trinity Church today. In the 1950s, members of Trinity Church petitioned members of the Baptist church to take over control of the old structure. When members of the Baptist church vetoed the idea, it spelled the end of the brick structure. In 1955, the windows of the church were removed and the structure made way for Dr. Blanchard's office (today the dental practice of Neil Solsburg) and a parking lot for Eagle Funeral Home.

YESTERDAY: Hudson has always loved a party. Here are images from Hudson's street fair, taken around 1907. The upper image shows the Bean Chamberlain display in front of the Cogswell House. Below are fairgoers walking through the displays on Church Street.

TODAY: The same view today, taken from Dr. Mathew Taylor's pony farm. In the one hundred-plus years between the images, trees have grown to obscure the cityscape.

Copyright © 2010 by W. G. Thompson House Museum

All rights reserved. No part of this book may be used or reproduced in any manner, including Internet usage, without the express written permission of the publisher, except in the case of brief quotations embodied in critical articles and reviews.

Published by
W. G. Thompson House Museum
101 Summit Street
Hudson, MI 49247

Book design by Lee Lewis Walsh, Words Plus Design, www.wordsplusdesign.com